TEEN LIFE™

FREQUENTLY ASKED QUESTIONS ABOUT

# Body Piercing and Tattooing

Sarah Sawyer

ROSEN
PUBLISHING®

New York

Published in 2009 by The Rosen Publishing Group, Inc.
29 East 21st Street, New York, NY 10010
www.rosenpublishing.com

**Library of Congress Cataloging-in-Publication Data**

Sawyer, Sarah.
Frequently asked questions about body piercing and
tattooing / Sarah Sawyer. — 1st ed.
    p. cm. — (FAQ: teen life)
Includes bibliographical references and index.
ISBN-13: 978–1–4042–1812–3 (library binding)
1. Body piercing—Juvenile literature. 2. Tattooing—
Juvenile literature.  I. Title.
GN419.25.S33 2009
391.6'5—dc22

                                        2007044385

*Manufactured in the United States of America*

# Contents

# WHY IS BODY MODIFICATION POPULAR TODAY?

Body modification in the form of tattooing and piercing is more popular in the United States than ever before. It is a trend that started spiking in the 1990s and has since grown steadily. In fact, according to a 2004 survey published in the *Journal of the American Academy of Dermatology*, 24 percent of American adults between the ages of eighteen and fifty have at least one tattoo. Among the variety of people who today proudly sport tattoos are the writer John Irving and the basketball player Lebron James. The Dixie Chicks have matching tattoos.

Although you must be at least eighteen years old to obtain a tattoo in most states, tattooing has become especially trendy among young people. Despite the growing popularity of tattooing, the decision to permanently alter your body is a serious one. You should never get a tattoo or piercing as a way to fit in or try out a passing

Some people prefer their tattoos small and have them applied where few will ever see them. Others get large, colorful tattoos that they display for all to see.

style or trend. The first step in making a wise decision about whether or not to get a modification is to be well informed about the benefits and risks associated with it.

# What Is Body Modification?

Any changes made to the body for spiritual, fashion, social, or personal reasons are known as body modifications. This umbrella term includes piercing, tattooing, earlobe stretching, branding, and cutting, as well as more unusual choices such as dental, facial, ocular, and breast implants. Even dramatic and life-changing procedures such as gender-reassignment surgery fall into the body modification category.

# Today's Tattoo Culture

It was during the 1980s that tattooing really began to take its place in mainstream America. Lyle Tuttle had been a driving force behind this movement, and he has since become its icon.

In 1960, Tuttle opened a small studio in San Francisco, called Lyle Tuttle Tattoo, above a Greyhound bus station in San Francisco. He said it was the spirit of the times that made society ripe for a tattoo revolution:

"Women's liberation put tattooing back on the map. With women getting a newfound freedom, they could get tattooed if they so desired. It increased and opened the market by 50 percent of the population . . . For three years I tattooed almost nothing but women [who] made tattooing a softer and kinder art form."

Lyle Tuttle, shown here, got his first tattoo at fourteen years old, in 1946. Tattoos now cover practically his entire body.

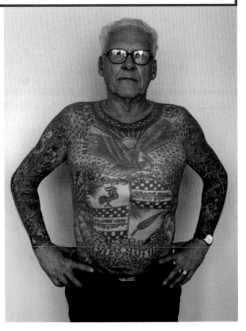

San Francisco in the 1960s was a hotbed for progressive thinking and revolutionary counterculture. One way the youth of the time expressed themselves about the issues of the day, like the war in Vietnam, the civil rights movement, and the sexual revolution, was to get tat-tooed. Throughout the decade, tattoos appeared on hippies and revolutionaries, many of whom later helped usher body art into mainstream society. Today, a Tuttle tattoo is quite sought after and highly admired, since he is considered the father of modern tattooing.

In the late 1970s and early 1980s, the punk movement embraced body modification in an effort to mock bourgeois society, popularizing multiple ear piercings and visible tattoos, especially among youths in England and the United States. Earrings became more common on men. By the early 1990s, multiple piercings were no longer shocking. It was not uncommon to see people of either gender with a row of earrings all along the outer

Body modification is more common now than ever. What do you think when you see someone with multiple tattoos and body piercings?

line of the ear. Like symbolic tribal associations made through the identification of certain body marks, punks and trendsetters were identifying members of their subculture by specific tattoos and piercings.

By the mid- to late 1990s, piercings and tattoos were showing up on pop stars, professional athletes, politicians, and many others. On young women, pierced tongues, hard ear cartilage, and belly buttons became popular. Pierced ears, noses, and eyebrows appeared on young men.

# WHAT ARE THE RISKS INVOLVED IN TATTOOING?

A tattoo is a permanent marking created by making a series of small puncture wounds, about one-eighth of an inch into the skin, with a needle or group of needles. Tattoo artists should be willing to discuss this process with you and answer any questions that you may have before you decide to go ahead with the procedure. You should seek tattoos only from fully trained and licensed tattoo artists. Also, anyone seeking a tattoo should first obtain a hepatitis B vaccination to safeguard against the spread of this one form of viral hepatitis.

## Your Tattooing Session

At the beginning of your session, you will be asked to show photo identification to prove you are at least eighteen years old, and you will need to sign a form declaring that you

This woman isn't sure what kind of tattoo she wants. To inspire such customers, tattoo parlors display flash, or design ideas, on their walls.

are healthy and not under the influence of drugs or alcohol. If you are underage, most tattoo artists will not work on you. Others may if you have a parent or guardian with you or a parent or guardian gives you written permission. Because laws governing licensed tattoo artists vary by state, these rules may be different depending on where you are.

You and your artist will discuss your tattoo, the process, and your design. You may want to look at flash (tattoo designs) in the studio, or you may have your own original idea for a tattoo.

Once everything is agreed upon, the tattoo artist will generally transfer the outline of the design onto your skin. Some artists suggest that you live with this drawn-on design for a few days as a test run before they permanently mark the skin.

The tattoo session begins with the artist washing his or her hands before cleaning the area of skin that will be tattooed. Wearing surgical gloves and sometimes covering his or her mouth and nose with a surgical mask, the artist opens a sterile, single-use needle, which is inserted into the tattoo machine. If the artist does not open the needle in front of you, then it may

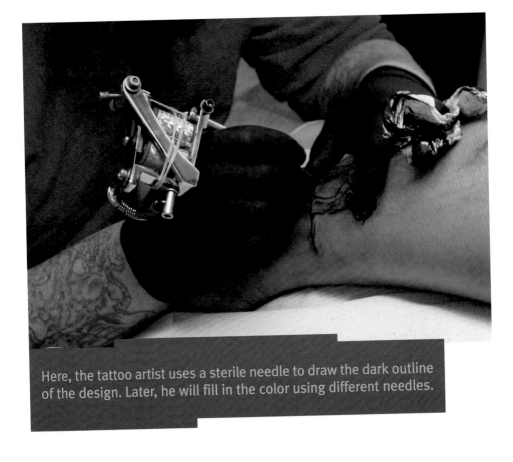

Here, the tattoo artist uses a sterile needle to draw the dark outline of the design. Later, he will fill in the color using different needles.

not be sterile. If this is the case, you should leave the shop immediately. All equipment used for the tattooing procedure should be sterilized in an autoclave—a machine specifically designed to sterilize medical tools and instruments.

Using the tattoo machine, the artist begins to etch the outline of the tattoo into your skin. As the outline is completed, it may be wiped with ointment and washed with soap and water. Any blood on the surface of the skin will be removed with a disposable towel.

Having completed the outline, the artist will open another set of sterile, single-use needles for filling in the design with colors. Smaller tattoos may be completed in one forty-five-minute session, but larger, more complicated tattoos may need to be completed in a series of sessions, each scheduled approximately four weeks apart. When a session is completed, the artist will wipe any blood away with ointment and a disposable towel and apply a bandage.

## Health Risks of Tattooing

Because applying a tattoo breaks the skin, there are a variety of associated risks. These include contracting blood-borne diseases, skin infections, scarring and keloid formation, and allergic reactions.

Blood-borne diseases such as HIV (the virus that causes AIDS), hepatitis C, hepatitis B, tuberculosis, and syphilis can all be transmitted by coming into contact with the blood of an infected person. Licensed tattoo artists are required to use only single-use needles to guard against the transmission of these diseases, but there is still some risk associated with coming into contact with equipment that is used to tattoo hundreds, if not thousands, of people.

## Hepatitis C

A 2001 study by the University of Texas Southwestern Medical Center suggested that there might be a correlation in the United States between the rise in popularity of tattoos and the increase in hepatitis C infections. Out of more than 600 patients surveyed, 22 percent who had tattoos were infected with hepatitis versus 3.5 percent of those without tattoos. The study further urged physicians to screen their tattooed patients for hepatitis C. According to Robert Haley, M.D., and coauthor of the study, "As far as I know, Texas is the only state that inspects tattoo parlors, even though hepatitis C can give you a fatal disease that can cut your life short by twenty or thirty years." It is now widely believed that people with tattoos are nine times more likely to be infected with hepatitis C than non-tattooed individuals.

## Bacterial Infections

Getting a tattoo can lead to a bacterial infection, which may be life threatening. According to the Centers for Disease Control and Prevention (CDC), some serious skin infections associated with tattooing are on the rise.

Health writers for Reuters reported in June 2006 that six outbreaks of the "superbug" methicillin-resistant *Staphylococcus aureus* (MRSA) had been traced to unlicensed tattoo artists in Kentucky, Ohio, and Vermont. According to Reuters, "MRSA

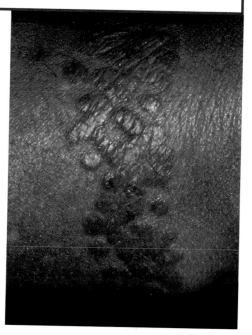

A rash broke out on this woman's wrist at the site of a tattoo. Allergies to tattoo inks are not uncommon.

infection typically manifests in abscesses or areas of inflammation on the skin, though it can also lead to more serious problems such as pneumonia, blood infections, or in some cases, necrotizing fasciitis, also referred to as the 'flesh-eating disease.'" The MRSA outbreaks affected more than forty people, six of whom got it from close contact with one of the tattooed individuals. Signs of skin infection may include redness, irritation, warmth, swelling, pus bumps, and discharge. If you see any of these signs on or around a new tattoo, you should seek immediate help from a medical professional.

## Other Risks

Tiny bumps forming within a tattoo may be scars, keloids, allergic reactions, or granulomas. Granulomas are a way the body reacts to deposited pigment. They are most common with red ink, but they have also been reported with blue and purple pigments. During an MRI (magnetic resonance imaging, a medical procedure that scans the body to examine internal organs), the iron in some tattoo pigments may be magnetized and it may move, leading to tingling or burning in the skin. The ink can also obscure the image produced by an MRI and, therefore, may hinder medical management.

# Tattoo Aftercare

In order to fight infection or further injury to the area, the bandage must stay on a fresh tattoo for at least twenty-four hours. During that time, it is important not to scratch the skin or pick at any scabs that might form. While scabs may look like an obstruction of the tattoo, they are only temporary and are an important part of the healing process. Picking at the scab can cause infection and scarring, which may alter the design of the tattoo.

Any redness or swelling of the newly tattooed area may be soothed by the application of an ice pack. Other care may include washing the area with soap and applying antibacterial ointments. Use soaps and ointments recommended and/or provided by the tattoo artist. Other chemicals, e.g., hydrogen peroxide and rubbing alcohol, are not recommended for soothing or cleaning freshly tattooed skin.

For a period of up to two weeks, your new tattoo may look glossy. This is a sign that the skin has not completely healed. In tattoo culture, this is called "fresh ink." Until that glossy look fades and the tone of the tattooed area begins to match the rest of your skin, it requires special care. Never get another tattoo before this condition fades.

## Personal or Aesthetic Risks

Tattoo designs may change over time. Not all pigment colors show well with all skin tones; for instance, light colors may not show on fair-skinned individuals and bright colors may look better on those with dark skin. Changes in the skin related to aging or stretching from pregnancy or weight gain, as well as from weight loss, will change a tattoo. Discuss inks and design durability with the tattoo artist before making a final decision as to where to place your tattoo.

It's possible that your feelings about your tattoo will change over time as your tastes mature. For example, you may not want a girlfriend's or boyfriend's name tattooed on your body because you might part ways. Or, as you enter college, you may wish you hadn't had your high school mascot tattooed on your arm. If you ever want to get a corporate job or join the military, you may wish you hadn't gotten a gang tattoo.

## Tattoo Removal

Never make a hasty decision to get a tattoo because you think that you can have it removed. While it is true that tattoos can be removed, it is important to remember that the process is very expensive, is quite painful, and does not leave the skin with a flawless appearance. In addition, some tattoo inks are more difficult to remove than others.

Tattoos are most often removed by laser surgery, a procedure performed by a dermatologic surgeon on an outpatient basis with local anesthesia. This means that you won't need to stay

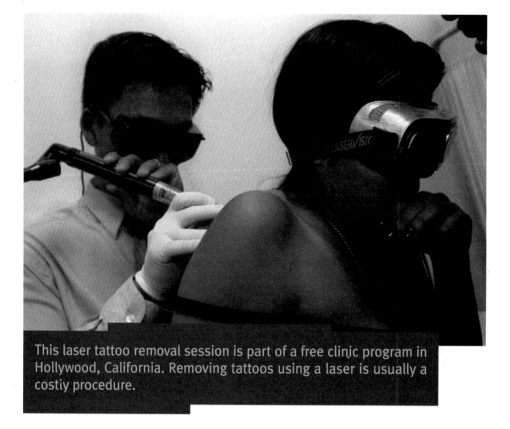

This laser tattoo removal session is part of a free clinic program in Hollywood, California. Removing tattoos using a laser is usually a costly procedure.

overnight and that the anesthesia will numb only the area where the tattoo is located. However, the procedure can be painful depending on the extent and site of the tattoo removal and the types of pigments that were used to create it. In addition, laser surgery is costly. A small tattoo that cost less than $100 to obtain might cost between $1,500 and $2,000 to remove, depending on the number of laser treatments needed.

Another method of tattoo removal is dermabrasion. A handheld mechanical unit or sterile sandpaper is used to abrade the surface and middle layers of the skin. Rotating (up to 33,000 rpm) wire brushes, diamond fraises, or serrated wheels attached to compact electric machines are available. Afterward, moist dressings are used until the area has healed.

A third option is surgical excision, in which a surgeon cuts out the tattoo with a scalpel and closes the wound with stitches. This method allows complete removal but always leaves a scar.

An alternative to tattoo removal is "inking over" an unwanted tattoo with a darker tattoo, leaving a denser, more intense-looking tattoo.

When deciding on an artist to help achieve a body modification, you should always ask questions beforehand. While making up your mind, consider asking the tattoo artist or skilled piercer the following questions:

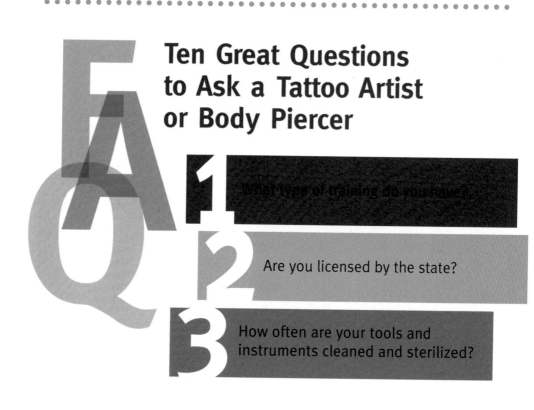

## Ten Great Questions to Ask a Tattoo Artist or Body Piercer

**1** What type of training do you have?

**2** Are you licensed by the state?

**3** How often are your tools and instruments cleaned and sterilized?

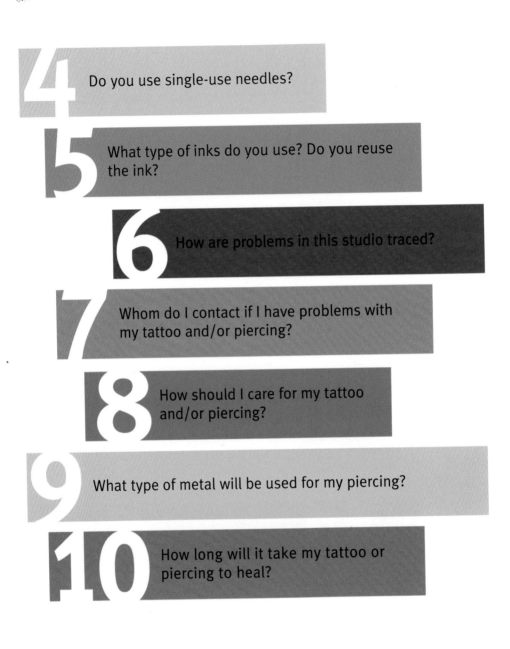

4 Do you use single-use needles?

5 What type of inks do you use? Do you reuse the ink?

6 How are problems in this studio traced?

7 Whom do I contact if I have problems with my tattoo and/or piercing?

8 How should I care for my tattoo and/or piercing?

9 What type of metal will be used for my piercing?

10 How long will it take my tattoo or piercing to heal?

# WHAT ARE THE RISKS INVOLVED IN PIERCING?

Any time the skin is broken, there is a risk of infection. The same risk holds true when you choose to get your body pierced. A piercing is simply a hole poked through body tissue with a needle and then fitted with jewelry. Although you may have friends who have done their own piercings or who have had piercings done by friends, these practices are not safe. Except for the piercing of the soft earlobe, the use of piercing guns is considered risky as blunt studs loaded onto a spring-loaded device may tear the skin and underlying tissue. The problem with reusable kits is that they are hard to sterilize. If a kit is for one use only, this is not a problem. A piercing should be done only by a licensed piercer. According to the Association of Professional Piercers, forty-three states currently have legislation "regarding personal criteria for the piercer, requirements

for the piercing establishment, and highly specific laws necessitating parental consent for the piercing of minors."

# Getting Pierced

Before getting a piercing, you need to choose your jewelry. While trendy and inexpensive body jewelry is available at shopping malls and fashion jewelry counters, it is better to buy the jewelry from your piercer. He or she can help you decide which styles and gauges (widths of wire) are appropriate for the

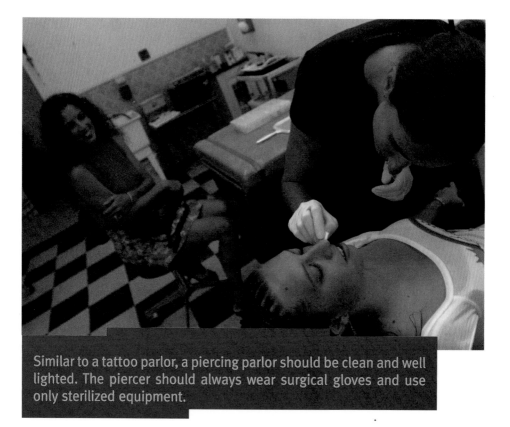

Similar to a tattoo parlor, a piercing parlor should be clean and well lighted. The piercer should always wear surgical gloves and use only sterilized equipment.

site and size of the piercing. The piercer will be likely to carry quality metals that won't cause an allergic reaction as your piercing heals. Suggested metals include surgical steel, solid 14-karat or 18-karat gold, niobium, titanium, or platinum.

Just like the forms you sign when you get a tattoo, you will have to sign paperwork stating that you are of age to be pierced and that you consent to the procedure. You will be asked to show identification with your photo, and if you are less than eighteen years old, your parent or guardian may need to provide permission in writing.

A small mark will be drawn on your skin where the piercing is to be placed. The piercer will wash his or her hands as well as the area of your body to be pierced before opening a small, sterile packet containing a single-use, stainless-steel needle. Some needles are used by hand and others are inserted into a piercing gun; the method depends on personal preference and the position of the piercing. All equipment should be sterilized in an autoclave. The piercer then makes a puncture wound and immediately slips the jewelry through the hole before washing away any blood. Depending on the location of the wound, the process is almost painless, though certain spots are more sensitive than others. Healing times vary and depend on the area pierced; for instance, the soft earlobe may take only six weeks to heal and the nipple up to six months, whereas the navel may take up to a year to heal.

# Health Risks of Piercing

"Doctors say that tongue and genital piercings can provide further channels for bacteria and viruses to enter the bloodstream after

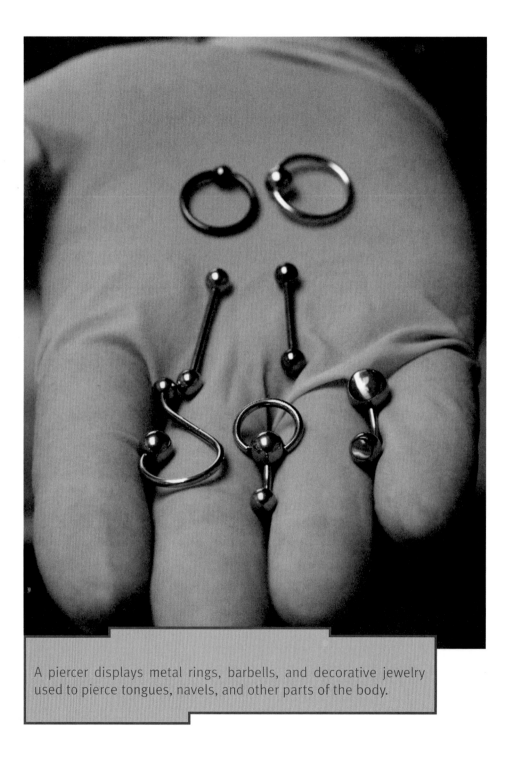

A piercer displays metal rings, barbells, and decorative jewelry used to pierce tongues, navels, and other parts of the body.

the piercing procedure," states a 2005 article in the *New York Times*. People who are pierced are constantly exposed to the risks of infection. In addition, genital piercing may increase the risks of sexually transmitted diseases like gonorrhea, herpes simplex, and HIV, since they may break condoms and tear flesh, further exposing a person to potentially infectious body fluids.

Piercing through the tongue makes people especially vulnerable to infection spreading from mouth fluids through the bloodstream or into the tissues of the neck. Experts have traced deadly infections of the vital organs back to tongue piercings. This is why doctors advise people, especially those with existing heart problems, to take antibiotics prior to and immediately after undergoing some piercing procedures. Most people, however, don't consult their doctors as part of their decision-making process.

## Piercing Aftercare

The person who does the piercing should discuss how to care for it and give you a sheet of paper with aftercare instructions. These generally include washing the area with antibacterial soap twice a day and may include rinsing the area with salt water. Listen carefully: getting a piercing can be overwhelming, and you may not remember all of the aftercare instructions when you get home. Just like when you get a tattoo, you should watch for signs of infection at the piercing site, like redness, irritation, swelling, warmth, or a puslike discharge. If you see any one of these signs, you should immediately consult a medical professional because infections can travel through the bloodstream and become even more health threatening. Depending on the location, a piercing can take several months to a year to heal. If you are concerned about a prolonged healing time, discuss various piercing locations and expected healing rates with a health professional.

An article in the *Journal of the American Medical Association* (JAMA) warns that improperly cleaned piercing equipment or jewelry can carry contaminants and lead to serious infections such as hepatitis. It recommends seeking fully trained piercers who use sterile, single-use equipment and have stringent cleaning policies.

The risk isn't over once the piercing session is finished. A medical study published in the *Journal of the American Academy of Dermatology* states that of seventy-one participants in a study measuring complications of body modifications, specifically piercing, 18 percent of them had complications lasting two or more weeks. Twenty-three percent of people with a mouth piercing had chipped or broken teeth as a result of living with their body jewelry in place. It is also possible that heavy-gauge body jewelry will tear the skin, ruining your piercing and giving your previously pierced skin a torn or forked look.

According to Dr. Scott Hammer, professor of medicine at Columbia College of Physicians and Surgeons, "One piercing in ten becomes infected. *Staphylococcus* bacteria, which can live on the skin and in the nose, is a frequent cause."

A piercing may close once the jewelry is removed, but this depends on the position and age of the piercing, the gauge of the jewelry, and the body chemistry of the person being pierced.

Just a few decades ago, piercings in the United States were usually done only to women's earlobes. Today, pierced noses and tongues are commonplace for both men and women.

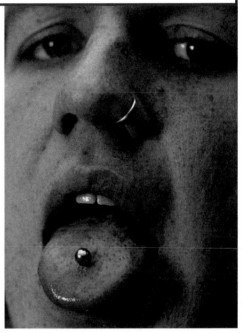

Many people develop a raised and thickened scar over a piercing after removing the jewelry. This is a natural part of the healing process, but some people find it unattractive.

# Stretching

Stretching is a prolonged and stylized method of piercing that results in the enlargement of a piercing or body part, usually the earlobes but occasionally the lips or other areas. It is done for aesthetic, social, and/or spiritual reasons. (In some places, stretching is called "gauging," a reference to the increasing widths of materials placed in the hole to stretch it.) A stretched piercing is often maintained with grommet-like jewelry, tapers, weights, and/or plugs. It may require months or years of careful attention to develop the desired shape.

The process involves inserting larger gauge jewelry into the pierced site incrementally over months or years. It is generally recommended to go up only one size per month. This is the best way to measure your stretching and monitor the process. Avoid using just any object to stretch a piercing because some objects may increase your chances of developing an infection. To ease the stretching process, use a water-based lubricant, or stretch after the heat from a shower or hot compress has made the skin more pliable.

Other objects for stretching may include tapers, which are horn-shaped objects made of metal, wood, glass, or bone, that begin at a comfortable gauge and gradually increase in diameter. Some people use tapers as a tool for inserting larger jewelry into a piercing, but they may be worn as jewelry. Weights may also

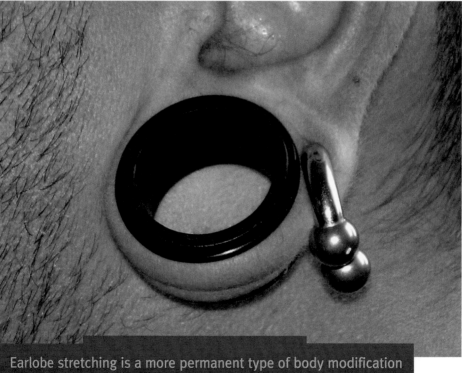

Earlobe stretching is a more permanent type of body modification than regular piercing. Stretching an earlobe to the degree shown in this photo takes place gradually, over a long time.

be used for stretching. Tiny metal weights are attached via a plug so that they stretch the piercing.

Another way to achieve a stretched earlobe is by scalpelling, a process by which the lobe is cut with a scalpel and a plug is inserted with a taper. No flesh is removed in this process. A sterile dermal punch, a surgical instrument like a common paper hole punch, can also be used to remove some flesh of the soft earlobe in order to accommodate plugs. (A paper hole punch cannot achieve this look safely or effectively.)

Stretching too quickly may result in painful, easily infected tearing and scarring. It may also cause a piercing blowout. A piercing blowout is when the skin of the ear grows over the jewelry. In this case, an unusual ridge of flesh, looking something like a lip, forms over the edge of the jewelry.

# Chapter four

## WHAT DOES YOUR BODY ART SAY ABOUT YOU?

Getting a tattoo or piercing can have an effect on your relationships with family, friends, and everyone you meet for the rest of your life. You've likely heard people say, "You never get a second chance to make a first impression." There's wisdom in that statement. People consider our appearances when they first meet us and use the information they gather to help them form an opinion. As people get to know us, they form more detailed impressions of our true selves, but that first impression is an important starting point.

## Mixed Messages

Your body modification sends messages to the people you meet. Different people will attach different meanings to those messages. While some people might see your

Understand that piercings and tattoos affect your overall appearance. This woman's radical haircut, unusual makeup, and daring fashion sense make her tattoos and piercings stand out even more.

piercing and think you are fashionable, hip, and adventurous, others will interpret your appearance as a statement against mainstream society. They will think that you embrace an alternative lifestyle. Others might think that your body modification is an indication that you engage in risky behaviors. Put more simply, having a body modification will get you "in" with some crowds and keep you on the fringes of others. You should consider the social implications of your body modifications before you make your decision to obtain them.

# In School

Some school dress codes prohibit visible body modifications. If your school is one of them, you could be forced to remove your jewelry or cover your tattoo during school hours. You might even be expelled.

If being home-schooled or dropping out of school in order to bypass a school dress code limits your abilities to meet your personal goals, you may want to weigh the personal importance of being modified against the importance of attaining a proper education. Whether it's right or wrong, having a body modification quickly becomes more than an aesthetic choice. It is important to note that school is not the end of these struggles. These issues follow many adults into the workplace.

# In the Workplace

One of the areas in which having a body modification is most challenging is in the workplace. If you've talked to professionals about your interest in a body modification, you've possibly heard someone say, "Oh, you'll never get a job with that!" Their concern for your future career is valid. While there is evidence that body modifications are becoming more common and acceptable in some situations, they are a far cry from fitting into the American standard of business casual. In many instances, your employer may ask you to cover visible tattoos or remove jewelry while you are working. This is absolutely legal. Employers are permitted to impose dress codes as long as they do not discriminate based on an employee's gender, race, skin color, ethnicity, religion, or age.

Some people will tell you that their workplace accepts tattoos and piercings. People who are employed in more casual establishments such as nightclubs, coffee shops, record stores, fitness clubs, and hair salons sometimes find their tattoos and piercings to be status quo.

# Changing Times

One employer that is changing its stand on hiring people with tattoos is the U.S. Army. Until recently, tattoos were permitted as long as a dress uniform could cover them. Recently, however, the Pentagon announced that it is changing its tune. Reacting to a changing youth culture and record-low recruiting totals, recruiters have begun to accept applicants with some neck and facial tattoos.

This policy is more liberal, but it is still far from "anything goes." A recent article in the *Los Angeles Times* offered the following excerpt from guidelines given to

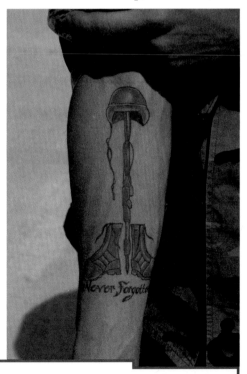

Tattoos, like this one honoring a friend who died in combat, are a longstanding tradition among soldiers in the armed forces of the United States.

recruiters by the Pentagon: "All tattoos that are on the neck that are not vulgar, profane, indecent, racist, or extremist, are authorized as long as it does not extremely degrade military appearance." The policy also forbids sexist tattoos, such as "those that advocate a philosophy that degrades or demeans a person based on gender."

# Body Modifications and Your Family

Your interest in tattoos and body piercing may or may not cause some conflict between you and your parents. Just as there are a wide variety of feelings about body modifications among young people, the reaction of parents can vary. Perhaps your parents have handed you the old line, "As long as you live under my roof, you'll do as I say," and they have completely forbidden you from getting any type of body modification. In that case, you may have a difficult road ahead. The best thing you can do, if you really want to make a case for your choice, is to do the following homework.

Learn everything you can about the body modification that sparks your interest. Are there any age restrictions to your choice, and if so, do you meet the age requirement? In other cases, would you first need your parents' permission? Think about why you want the tattoo or piercing. Have you given your decision significant thought? Can you thoroughly explain your interests to your parents? If so, sit down with them and discuss your decision rationally and calmly. Explain that you have researched the pros and cons of getting the body modification and offer examples of your newfound knowledge on the subject.

Some parents will be receptive to your idea of getting a tattoo or body piercing. Others will do all they can to talk you out of it.

Chances are, most parents will be more receptive when they learn that you have given your decision serious thought. Above all, learn about all of the risks associated with the procedures and share your findings with your parents. Together, you can make an informed choice.

# Making Decisions

Most of us have some natural tendencies when it comes to making decisions. Some people make risky decisions hoping for the best possible outcome, while others avoid taking on the challenges of decision making in hopes of avoiding bad results. Some of us like to stick to safe patterns of behavior, while others jump headfirst into any challenge that catches the eye, without spending much time thinking about the consequences. Some people let the groups they belong to (or want to belong to) make decisions for them, while others put off making decisions altogether and accept whatever results fall their way.

None of these decision-making styles are entirely bad. There are good and bad aspects to all of them. Still, none of them are a substitute for a well-planned, carefully thought-out decision. In this section, we'll look at some processes that can help you make a satisfying and responsible choice about body modifications.

## Gaze into Your Future

Before you make any big decisions, take a moment to remember what you liked when you were ten years old. Now think about yourself today. How would you answer the same questions now? Chances are that your answers today are completely different from the answers you gave at ten years of age. Notice any differences or similarities in both sets of answers. The point is that people mature and their tastes change over time.

Keep in mind as you navigate the rest of your decision-making process that you are a growing, changing person. Spend time trying to decide truthfully if the body modification you want today will feel right to you on your wedding day, at a job interview, on a crowded beach, during a religious service, or when you meet your child's kindergarten teacher for the first time.

# Gather Information

Read everything you can find on the topic. Look through magazines and Web sites, and don't be afraid to gather information from the people you know who have some experience. They can be among your most valuable teachers.

Information gathered from friends, or from stories told by friends, is called anecdotal information. While not always the most accurate information, it can play an important part in making a healthy decision.

If you have close friends or acquaintances with body modifications, talk with them about their choices. Ask them what prompted them to have the modification. Ask about the procedure and healing process. Ask them about their friends' and family's reactions to their choice. Ask them about their own satisfaction with their decision. Listen carefully to all of the answers, but keep in mind that sometimes people, especially young people, put on a brave face in front of others. They may play down the pain that they felt during the procedure or gloss over some negative reactions.

# Zooming In

As your knowledge of body modifications grows, you may notice that your interest starts to narrow. You may find yourself very interested in a certain modification, design, color, placement, jewelry, or general style. You may start to think this is the kind of modification you'd like to have yourself. If so, you're ready to develop a focus question.

Developing a focus question simply means defining the question you are asking yourself in this decision-making process. As you think of a question, keep it simple. Your question can be as simple as, "Is a tongue piercing right for me?"

If you're having trouble narrowing down your focus question, you might want to start with a group of smaller questions. Your main question could be, "Is a body modification right for me?" As you kick that question around, you might want to list the types of body modifications that catch your interest. Next to each possibility, list some advantages and disadvantages of each. Keep this list with you. Add thoughts to your list as they occur to you during the day.

After time, you may notice that one or two possibilities recur frequently or rise to the top of your list. Those winning points of interest can become your focus question. Once you have a focus question, write it down on a piece of paper and get ready for some well-organized, effective, mature decision making.

## Digging Deeper

Some people like to make a list of pros (reasons for making a certain decision) and cons (reasons against making a certain decision). Often, people put one list on one side of a piece of notebook paper and the other list on the other side of the page.

The list can be used many ways. Sometimes, one side of the paper will have many more reasons than the other. At other times, the reasons on one side of the paper seem much more important than on the other. Still other times, the lists line up one way, but your heart leads you strongly in another direction. The lists aren't the final say; they're just a tool to help you see what you really think and feel about a certain set of options.

It's wise to do this process over a period of time. Doing it in one sitting might just tell you what decision you would make in the moment. Sometimes, putting a list away and revisiting it in a few days, weeks, or months can make the process more effective. If a body modification sounds exciting while you're gearing up for a goth festival but feels less attractive when you're thinking about the prom or your wedding day, then you have not yet settled on your final decision. If you look at your list every day for six months

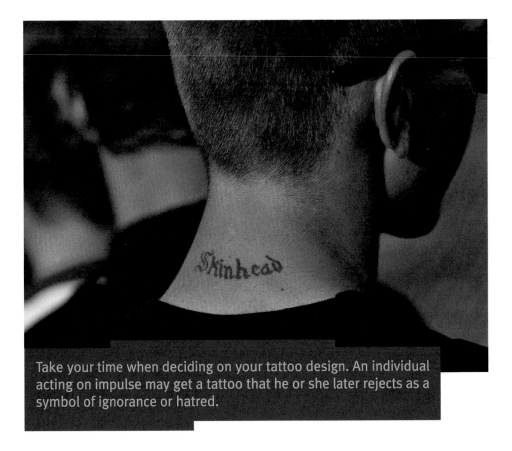

Take your time when deciding on your tattoo design. An individual acting on impulse may get a tattoo that he or she later rejects as a symbol of ignorance or hatred.

and agree with your decision every time, then you may be finished thinking it over. However, if your list looks different when you're in a different mood or in a different place in your life, then you've probably not settled on your final decision.

# Myths and Facts

 **You can pierce your own body with an ice cube, a safety pin, and a potato.**

Fact ➻ Home piercing is unsafe and not recommended. Even the use of piercing kits carries a greater risk of infection and tearing than having your piercing done by a licensed, skilled body artist. Also, avoid having anything pierced (or tattooed) at potentially unlicensed establishments such as at flea markets, carnivals, boardwalk venders, fairs, or similar facilities.

**White gold is one of the safest metals for body jewelry.**

Fact ➡ Fourteen-karat yellow gold, titanium, niobium, platinum, surgical-grade stainless steel, or a dense low-porosity plastic such as Tygon are unlikely to spark allergic reactions. Nickel and cobalt, which are ingredients in a lot of jewelry, including expensive white gold, cause allergic reactions more than other metals do.

 **Once you take your jewelry out, your piercing will heal over and disappear.**

Fact ➡ It is possible that your piercing will develop a thick, raised scar as it heals. Some people even develop keloids. If you stretch your piercing, you should remember that stretching may be permanent. Some people notice that their piercing closes up slightly, or entirely, when jewelry is removed, but this does not happen with all piercings.

 **A tattoo artist will tattoo any area of the body that you desire.**

Fact ➡ Many tattoo artists won't tattoo certain areas of the body, such as the palms of the hands, the fingers, and the bottoms of the feet. Others have even more stringent restrictions, and some states have laws forbidding tattooing on certain parts of the body, such as the face, near the eyes, or the fingertips. Check with your area artists for specific information.

Myth

**Even though I just got a tattoo a few months ago, I can still donate blood during the annual blood drive at my school.**

**Fact** → According to the American Association of Blood Banks, blood donors must wait at least twelve months after getting a tattoo or a piercing before donating blood, unless it is applied by a state-regulated entity with sterile needles and non-reused ink.

# WHAT ARE GOOD ALTERNATIVES TO PIERCING AND TATTOOING?

Making a decision about whether or not to get a tattoo or piercing takes time, and the process can be frustrating if you want to change your look right away. If you need to feel funky by Friday but are just beginning to sift through the decision-making process, it's possible that a less permanent addition to your appearance would do the trick. In some instances, you may even prefer the temporary nature of one of the following body art options.

## Bindi

Maybe you've noticed the red dots some Indian women wear on their foreheads? In Hindi culture, the red dot is made from a mixture of spices and powders, such as vermillion and saffron, which is applied like makeup and worn by married women. This red dot signifies their status as matriarchs and is believed to bring them good luck and prosperity.

Variations of this dot have become somewhat fashionable in Western culture. In America, wearing a bindi doesn't need to signify marriage; it can just be worn for adornment. (Although, if you're going to borrow this tradition, it's probably wise to learn a little something about it.) People who wear bindi for fashion often opt for a sticker bindi rather than applying it with paint or cosmetics. Sticker bindi are inexpensive, easily applied, easily removed, and available in a variety of colors, shapes, and styles. Some have crystals, sequins, and tiny beads.

They're a no-risk way to enjoy a trend and make an individual statement. With a little creativity, you can find colors, shapes, and placements that are uniquely yours.

# Mehndi

Mehndi are long-lasting and intricate designs painted on the skin with paste made from henna leaves, which are ground into a powder and mixed with liquids such as eucalyptus oil. Mehndi (also called mehendi or mehandi) has a long history of being used in places like the Middle East, North Africa, and South Asia. Like a tattoo, henna is applied to any body part, although it is traditionally found on the hands, the feet, and sometimes the face in ornate designs. The henna paste is painted on the skin with a brush or penlike bottle. The paste dries over a period of several hours and is then peeled off, leaving an auburn-colored design on the skin.

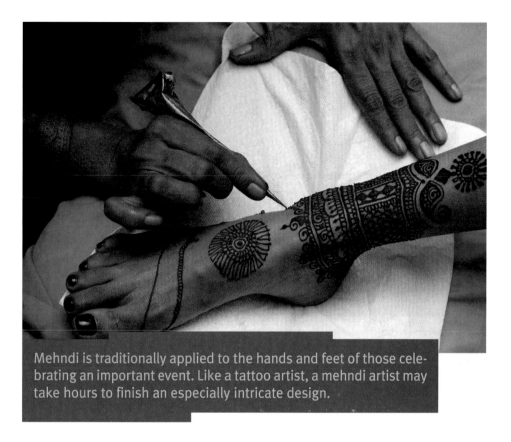

Mehndi is traditionally applied to the hands and feet of those celebrating an important event. Like a tattoo artist, a mehndi artist may take hours to finish an especially intricate design.

While tattoos are permanent because the ink is injected deep into the skin, henna merely dyes the top layers of skin, which are naturally shed over time, making it possible for you to experience up to four weeks of the mehndi without committing to a permanent design.

## Temporary Tattoos

Temporary tattoos have come a long way since they could be found on the insides of bubblegum wrappers. Today, a range of very convincing, colorful, and fashionable designs are available in trendy shops and online.

Wet-application temporary tattoos and airbrushed tattoos are quite beautiful, painless, and possible to change as frequently as your moods allow. They can be a great quick fix for someone teetering on the edge of a snap decision or a nice addition to your cosmetics for a special party or outing, especially for those of you who are underage. Experimenting with temporary tattoos may also help you decide whether or not a real tattoo is right for you. You might decide that a tattoo is not right for you after experiencing a similar temporary design for a few days.

Body painting is a good way to experience what it is like to have a large, colorful tattoo. Unlike a tattoo, however, it doesn't require a commitment you might later regret.

# Hairstyle

If you're looking to make a bold statement with your appearance, you might consider a dramatic haircut or alternative hair color. If you're naturally blonde, you can simply wash in some midnight blue or cupcake pink and have a fun, attention-getting fashion accessory for the next few weeks. (Be sure to use a temporary hair color product for this option.) If you want to cultivate a more goth or punk look, black hair dye is an effective and time-honored classic. Again, be sure to try a wash-in product rather than a permanent dye.

Not only will your new hair look fantastic, but it's also a great way to see if you really like attracting attention from strangers with your appearance.

# Magnetic Jewelry

Those of you who are curious about nose or ear piercing might want to first try magnetic jewelry to experiment with similar looks. It's a low-cost, painless, and risk-free way to add a little extra sparkle when you feel like a change. And parents who object to an alternative piercing might be willing to discuss your desire for a nose ring after they've adjusted to your new appearance.

# Non-Piercing Jewelry

Another low-cost, risk-free alternative to body piercing is to try non-piercing jewelry as a precursor or substitute for a piercing. It's an almost perfect solution for the under-sixteen set whose parents refuse to sign for a piercing. Non-piercing jewelry allows you to attach a metal ring to your eyebrow, nose, lip, or other areas. The rings stay on when gently pinched close. They are a much lower-risk way to get the same look, and nobody will know the difference!

# Chapter Six

## WHAT ELSE SHOULD I KNOW ABOUT GETTING A TATTOO?

If you've decided to get a tattoo, you'll need to pick a design. If there's a tattoo parlor near you, it might be a good idea to stop in and look at flashes (the paper drawings of tattoo designs that hang on the walls in many studios) or ask to see a portfolio. This will give you an idea of practical design styles. Resist the urge to make an impulse decision, since the design you choose will be with you for the rest of your life. You'll want to make sure that you like it, that it represents you well, and that it is meaningful to you.

If you're planning to have a set of tattoos or an entire sleeve done over the course of your life, this is a good time to begin to think about a theme so that your collection of tattoos has enough commonality between them to match. (For example, some themes might include anime characters, Celtic designs, fantasy characters and fairies, or a rockabilly theme with pin-up girls and Las Vegas icons.)

# Anatomy of a Tattoo

The artists at Texas Tattoo offer this description of the anatomy of a tattoo in their frequently asked questions section. "A tattoo is made up of several different components. The three major ones are the outline, the black shading, and the color. Each of these requires a different machine setup and technique. The outlines should be consistent in thickness and definition. The shading should be smooth and have good transition from dark to light. The color should be laid in solid without 'holidays' [breaks]. These qualities combined should result in a tattoo that will stand the test of time."

A strong, well-articulated tattoo originates from a simple, uncluttered design. When you are considering certain designs, keep in mind the types of drawings you used to see in coloring books. Coloring book images have clear outlines, are usually limited to one or two easily recognizable icons, have limited detailing, and make clear the difference between areas to be shaded or colored and outlined borders.

Once you've gotten an idea of the types of designs that work as body art, start keeping an eye out for design material in the world around you. Magazine art, stationery, graphic T-shirts, stickers, doodles by friends, and other people's body art can offer a wealth of inspiration.

This dragon tattoo shows off all three main components of a good tattoo: sharp outlines, smooth black shading, and bright and attractive coloring.

If you find a design that is even close to what you want, it's wise to bring a picture of it to potential tattoo artists. This will help the artist re-create the design in the drafting stage. This is an important step! Have you ever gone to a salon for a haircut, described the style of your dreams to your stylist, and then left the salon with something completely different than what you imagined? Stylists, piercers, and tattoo artists are talented, but they are not mind readers. Having something that displays the design or style that you intend can go a long way toward bridging any communication gap, ultimately ensuring that you get the design you want.

It's also possible that the artist you have in mind will see your design choice and refer you to another artist. This doesn't mean that he or she doesn't like you or your design. It's simply that every artist has his or her own style, talent, and ability, and some artists are a better fit for your needs. If this happens, meet with the recommended artist. You may be very glad you did.

# Finding a Body Artist

Once you've located a few artists who do the kind of work you're looking for, see if you can visit their space or speak with them before setting up an appointment. It is important that you feel comfortable with the artist and the space and that he or she is properly trained and licensed. Also, examine the space: Is it clean? Are the restrooms clean? Has it been inspected by health officials? Look for certificates on the wall and note the inspection dates.

If you have a friend who is getting a tattoo or piercing, going along to his or her session will give you a good idea as to whether or not this is something you'd like for yourself. Keep in mind, however, that not all parlors will let friends and/or family attend the session. In some cases, it's actually against state law for anyone else to be present.

The Alliance of Professional Tattooists' Web site offers the following advice for people choosing a tattoo artist: "Your concerns are twofold. You need to find an artist whose work you like and who will work on you safely. Ask people where they got tattooed, especially if you really like the work you see. Ask to see photographs of the artist's work. Most often, the pictures will have been taken right after the work was completed, so redness and swelling are common. In spite of that, there are things you can learn. Are the lines clean and smooth, or broken and jagged? Do they meet up? Does the artist work in the style you are looking for? Taking time to check out a few artists and shops will ensure that you are happy with your results."

Don't settle for just any tattoo artist. Search until you find one who has professional standards and who clearly takes pride in his or her work.

# Knowledge Is Power

Only informed consumers can make informed choices. Before deciding on any particular tattoo artist, you should consider asking him or her the following questions:

- Is your equipment reusable?
- Do you use an autoclave to sterilize your reusable equipment?
- Do you use separate disposable and prepackaged sterile needles for each client?

➤ Do you use nonreusable ink?

➤ Do you wear disposable gloves during the procedure?

➤ What kind of training do you have? Is there a certificate available?

➤ Are you licensed by the state?

➤ What are the state or local requirements for inspection at this shop?

➤ Are your needles sterile and disposed of properly?

## Ask About Your Session

Once you've found a parlor and artist that seem like a good fit for you, ask about a session. You'll want to ask about his or her pricing (keep in mind that body modification sessions can be very expensive, though some artists will negotiate their fees). It's OK to ask him or her if there's "wiggle room" in his or her pricing, but you need to be ready to accept the fact that he or she may not budge. Also, there's nothing wrong with telling him or her that you need to save up for a session, if indeed you do. Just tell him or her that you'll call when you're able to pay for the session.

Just as you tip waiters and hairdressers, it's expected that you will tip your body modification artist. The general rule is a minimum of 10 percent of the price of your modification, and 20 to 25 percent if you found the work excellent. Keep this in mind as you budget for your modification.

If you find yourself questioning your decision once you've laid plans, it is absolutely OK to cancel or postpone your session. Don't worry about what people think; it is likely that deep down they

If you take the right approach, a tattoo or piercing can be an interesting bit of self-expression that you will be satisfied with for a long time.

will respect you for making a decision that's right for you.

## Prepare for Your Session

As your appointment gets closer, reread the chapter of this book that discusses what to expect from your session. Refresh your mind about the risks and complications associated with the body modification you've decided upon so you can ask appropriate questions. Make sure you meet all the age, health, and other requirements of your body modification studio prior to your arrival. Also, make sure you and your family are on the same page regarding permission for your modification. You want as few surprises and stressors on your session day as possible.

Finally, have a ride to and from your session. You may be too distracted to drive afterward. You may be just fine, but there's no need to risk it. Enlist a supportive and reliable friend or relative as your chauffeur for the day.

**anesthesia**  Loss of sensation of pain.

**autoclave**  A machine that uses steam at a high temperature to sterilize surgical instruments and tools.

**bourgeois**  Social class equated with the middle class.

**counterculture**  Cultural group that acts in opposition to the mainstream culture.

**dermatology**  The branch of medicine that specializes in the diagnosis and treatment of diseases of the skin, hair, nails, and mucous membranes.

**flash**  Selection of tattoo designs that hang on walls of tattoo parlors.

**fresh ink**  A term that describes a new tattoo, or one where the ink appears glossy.

**granulomas**  Nodules of inflamed human tissue.

**hepatitis**  A viral disease involving inflammation of the liver. Scientists now know there is a higher incidence of hepatitis among people who have tattoos.

**keloid**  A special type of scar that results in an overgrowth of tissue at the site of a healed skin injury. Certain individuals are predisposed to form keloids.

**mehndi**  The application of intricate temporary designs on the body, especially the hands and feet, with a henna paste. Mehndi originated in countries in North Africa, the Middle East, and South Asia.

**modify** To alter or change.

**necrotizing fasciitis** Also called the flesh-eating disease, a rare infection that destroys skin and the soft tissue beneath it.

**niobium** Lustrous light-grey metal often used to make jewelry.

**punk** Subculture begun in the 1970s that rejected mainstream culture. Punks were known by their distinctive appearance, which often featured piercings and tattoos.

**sterile** Free from germs or bacteria.

**syphilis** Blood-borne disease that damages the heart, brain, eyes, and bones.

# Information

Alliance of Professional Tattooists, Inc.

9210 S. Highway 17-92

Maitland, FL 32751

(407) 831-5549

Web site: http://www.safe-tattoos.com

The Alliance of Professional Tattooists, Inc., is a nonprofit, educational organization that was founded in 1992 to address health and safety issues facing the tattoo industry.

American Society for Dermatologic Surgery (ASDS)

5550 Meadowbrook Drive, Suite 120

Rolling Meadows, IL 60173

(847) 956-0900

Web site: http://www.asds.net

The American Society for Dermatologic Surgery was founded in 1970 to promote excellence in dermatologic surgery and foster the highest standards of patient care.

Association of Professional Piercers

P.O. Box 1287

Lawrence, KS 66044

(888) 888-1277

Web site: http://www.safepiercing.org

The Association of Professional Piercers is dedicated to

the dissemination of health and safety information related to body piercing to piercers, health care providers, and the public.

Body Art Supply, Inc.
4233 SE 182nd Avenue, #169
Gresham, OR 97030
(888) 994-3662
Web site: http://www.bodyartsupply.com
  Body Art Supply specializes in safe, low-cost alternatives to permanent tattooing and piercing, including tattoo transfers, decals, henna, and magnetic earrings.

National Tattoo Association, Inc.
485 Business Park Lane
Allentown, PA 18109
Web site: http://www.nationaltattooassociation.com
  The National Tattoo Association was founded in 1976 to heighten awareness about tattooing as a contemporary art form. It has since become an organization dedicated to the advancement in quality, safety standards, and professionalism in the tattooing community.

Professional Tattoo Artists Guild
27 Mt. Vernon Avenue, P.O. Box 1374
Mt. Vernon, NY 10550
(914) 668-2300
  This organization has supported professional tattoo artists since 1976.

Tattoo Directory
1599 Superior Avenue, B-3
Costa Mesa CA 92627
(949) 548-3878
(888) 995-3500
E-mail: tattoodirectory@sbcglobal.net
Web site: http://www.tattoodirectory.com
This is a worldwide directory of tattoo artists, tattoo studios, piercers, permanent cosmetics, organizations, calendar of events, and vendors and supplies.

## Web Sites
Due to the changing nature of Internet links, Rosen Publishing has developed an online list of Web sites related to the subject of this book. This site is updated regularly. Please use this link to access the list:

http://www.rosenlinks.com/faq/bpat

# For Further Reading

Demello, Margo. *Bodies of Inscription: A Cultural History of the Modern Tattoo Community.* Durham, NC: Duke University Press, 2000.

Gilbert, Steve. *The Tattoo History Source Book.* New York, NY: Powerhouse Books, 2004.

Green, Terisa, Ph.D. *Ink: The Not-Just-Skin-Deep Guide to Getting a Tattoo.* New York, NY: NAL Trade, 2006.

Groning, Karl. *Decorated Skin: A World Survey of Body Art.* New York, NY: Thames & Hudson, 2002.

Mason, Paul. *Need to Know Body Piercing and Tattooing* (Need to Know). Portsmouth, NH: Heinemann Library, 2004.

Mifflin, Margot. *Bodies of Subversion: A Secret History of Women and Tattoo.* New York, NY: Powerhouse Books, 2001.

Parry, Albert. *Tattoo: Secrets of a Strange Art.* Mineola, NY: Dover Publications, 2006.

Winkler, Kathleen. *Tattooing and Body Piercing: Understanding the Risks* (Teen Issues). Berkeley Heights, NJ: Enslow Publishers, 2002.

## About the Author

Sarah Sawyer is a writer living in Kansas City, Missouri. This is the fifth teen-interest title she has written for Rosen Publishing.

## Photo Credits

Cover © www.istockphoto.com/Roberta Osborne; pp. 5, 12, 28, 31, 45, 46, 51, 53 Shutterstock.com; p. 7 © Donald Weber/Getty Images; p. 8 © Yellow Dog Productions/Stone/Getty Images; p. 11 © Tim Boyle/Getty Images; p. 15 © Dr. P. Marazzi/Photo Researchers, Inc.; p. 18 © Dan Callister/Getty Images; p. 22 © Greg Urquiaga/Contra Cost Times/Zuma Press; pp. 24, 27 © AP Images; p. 33 © www.istockphoto.com/Jeff Hower; p. 35 © Ellen B. Senisi/The Image Works; p. 39 © Steve Starr/Corbis; p. 55 © www.istockphoto.com/Markus Thomas.

Designer: Evelyn Horovicz; Editor: Christopher Roberts
Photo Researcher: Amy Feinberg